D0862094

Social Security Revisited

J. W. Van Gorkom

American Enterprise Institute for Public Policy Research
Washington, D.C.

J. W. Van Gorkom is chairman of the board of Trans Union Corporation and a member of the Quadrennial Advisory Council on Social Security.

Library of Congress Cataloging in Publication Data

Van Gorkom, Jerome W.   1917–
   Social security revisited.

   (AEI studies ; 241)
   1.   Social security—United States.   I.   Title.
II.   Series: American Enterprise Institute for Public
Policy Research.   AEI studies ; 241.
HD7125.V33   368.4'00973   79-15456
ISBN 0-8447-3344-X

AEI Studies 241

© 1979 by American Enterprise Institute for Public Policy Research,
Washington, D.C. All rights reserved. No part of this publication may
be used or reproduced in any manner whatsoever without permission
in writing from the American Enterprise Institute except in the case of
brief quotations embodied in news articles, critical articles, or reviews.

The views expressed in the publications of the American Enterprise Institute
are those of the authors and do not necessarily reflect the views of the staff,
advisory panels, officers, or trustees of AEI.

"American Enterprise Institute" is the registered service mark of the
American Enterprise Institute for Public Policy Research.

Printed in the United States of America

CONTENTS

801188

LIBRARY
ALMA COLLEGE
ALMA, MICHIGAN

INTRODUCTION

The social security system was created in 1935 in the depths of the Great Depression. It was originally intended to provide a basic minimum income for persons who could no longer work and was to be financed by a payroll tax that would, in essence, force covered workers to save for their old age.

Since its creation, the system has expanded enormously and now covers more than 90 percent of all workers. It has been patched, adjusted, and modified many times. It is now supplemented by other supportive programs to assist the retired, including private pension systems covering roughly 45 percent of all workers. Vast changes have occurred in the country's economy and in our society since the inception of the social security system. It is clearly time to reappraise the entire system without commitment to the past and to explore its underlying philosophy in the light of today's and tomorrow's realities.

Before anyone can decide how the system should work, he must start with a clear understanding of how the system now works. Not one person in a thousand, literally, has a thorough comprehension of the present system, despite the fact that 110 million workers pay social security taxes, and some 34 million are drawing benefits. Chapter 1 explains in some detail how the system works. Chapter 2 contains a critique of the system and suggests some changes.

1
The System as It Stands

The social security system is made up of three elements:

- Old Age and Survivors Insurance (OASI), as is well known, provides benefits for the retired worker. What is less well known is that this part of the system also provides substantial benefits for a worker's dependents and survivors.

- Disability Insurance (DI) provides income for a disabled worker and also for his dependents.

- Medicare (HI) helps meet medical expenses of persons after age sixty-five and of some younger disabled workers.

The first two elements are grouped together and referred to as OASDI. The benefits of OASDI are related to the earnings of the individual worker.

This study will *not* consider Medicare in any detail because it is a totally separate system, it serves an entirely different purpose, and its benefits bear no relation to the earnings of the worker. In fact, the combining of Medicare and OASDI is questionable at best.

Substantial changes in the OASDI system were made by Congress in 1977, but some of these changes did not become effective until January 1, 1979.[1] In the main, this study will consider the system as it has existed since that date so as to avoid the needless complication

---

[1] Public Law 95–216, 95th Congress, 1st Session, December 20, 1977, 91 Stat. 1509–1565. For a summary of the new law, see Colin D. Campbell, *The 1977 Amendments to the Social Security Act* (Washington, D.C.: American Enterprise Institute, 1978); and Robert J. Myers, "Social Security's Financial Woes Substantially Solved," *Edward H. Friend and Company, Quarterly Newsletter*, Washington, D.C., vol. 2, no. 3 (Summer/Fall 1977), and vol. 2, no. 4 (Winter 1977/1978).

of explaining both the old and the new systems. There are also transitional periods provided in the 1977 amendments for some of the changes, but these will usually be ignored in order to concentrate on broad underlying principles.

How OASDI Benefits Are Financed

Money to pay the benefits of OASDI is derived from a payroll tax levied on the earnings of some 110 million persons in the United States. The vast majority of federal civilian employees and about 30 percent of the employees of state and local governments comprise the only sizable group of workers not covered by the system. The tax is paid equally by the employer and by the employee, with the self-employed paying a tax equal to about 75 percent of the sum of the two.

Originally the OASDI tax was 1 percent on both employer and employee, payable on only the first $3,000 of annual earnings. Over the years the rate has been raised periodically on an ad hoc basis to the current 5.08 percent, making a combined tax of 10.16 percent split equally between employer and employee. The self-employed pay a tax of 7.05 percent. In 1979 the tax is paid on all earnings up to a maximum of $22,900 per year. In the coming years the tax rate and the maximum amount of earnings subject to tax are scheduled to rise as shown in Table 1.

To compute the full social security tax that is deducted from the worker's pay, the figures above would have to be increased by the Medicare tax, which is currently 1 percent and which will rise gradually to 1.45 percent by 1986.

The OASDI tax is levied on the first dollar of earnings up to the maximum amount. There are no deductions, exemptions, or exclusions as are provided in the personal income tax. As a result, the tax can create a heavy burden on low paid workers. For example, a worker with a wife and two children and who earns $5,200 a year will pay no income taxes, but he must pay over $250 in OASDI taxes, and over $300 if Medicare is included. For such a person whose income is so close to the poverty level, this tax payment means the sacrifice of necessities rather than the forgoing of luxuries. It is true that he is buying a great deal of protection for his future with these tax payments, particularly since the low paid worker receives substantially more protection for his tax dollar than does the high paid worker. Nevertheless, the tax payment can mean a great sacrifice for him and for his family.

TABLE 1
Social Security Tax Rates for OASDI as Scheduled in 1977 Amendments

Year	OASDI Tax Rate Paid by Both Employer and Employee (percent)	Tax Rate Paid by Self-employed (percent)	Maximum Earnings Subject to OASDI Tax (dollars)
1978	5.05	7.10	17,700
1979	5.08	7.05	22,900
1980	5.08	7.05	25,900
1981	5.35	8.00	29,700
1982–1984	5.40	8.05	—[a]
1985–1989	5.70	8.55	—[a]
1990	6.20	9.30	—[a]

[a] After 1981 the maximum rises in accord with national average wages.
Source: Public Law 95–216, 95th Congress, 1st Session, December 20, 1977, 91 Stat. 1512–1513.

Congress recognized this problem and created the earned income credit to rectify it. This device provides for certain taxpayers an income tax credit of 10 percent of all earned income up to $5,000. The credit is gradually reduced as income rises above $6,000 and it disappears above $10,000. The credit is refundable so that if a worker makes $3,000 and owes no income tax he receives a check from the Treasury for $300. One of the stated purposes of the credit is indirectly to refund part or all of the OASDI taxes the worker has paid.

The OASDI system is a blend of individual equity and social adequacy, and the former is frequently sacrificed to the latter. For example, the tax rate is the same for everyone, regardless of the protection and benefits one may receive. Thus, the married person with two children pays the same tax as a single person with identical earnings, and yet the married person receives additional protection for his wife and children that the single person does not receive. In the same vein, because of the way in which benefits are computed, the low paid worker receives substantially higher benefits and protection for his tax dollar than the high paid employee.

Although the OASDI tax is frequently described as regressive, this is inaccurate when considered together with benefits, because OASDI benefits are very progressive. As discussed in a later section, the lowest paid worker receives three times as much benefit

3

for his tax dollar as does the highest paid worker. This pronounced progressivity of the benefits offsets the regressivity of the tax itself. Whether the combination is sufficiently progressive is unanswerable, because there is no known standard of adequate progressivity.

When a private insurance company issues a retirement or disability policy, it charges premiums based on the estimated benefits to be paid *to the insured.* These actuarially computed premiums are collected and invested during the working life of the insured. The premiums and the income earned from their investment form a reserve fund from which the future benefits will be paid.

The OASDI system is financed on an entirely different system called current cost financing. Instead of premiums, the system collects payroll taxes, but they are not accumulated and invested. As soon as the payroll taxes are received, they are disbursed as benefits to persons already retired or disabled. Only a very small contingency fund is maintained. Nothing remotely approaching a full reserve fund exists, and therefore money to pay the benefits of today's workers must come from future generations of taxpayers.

The most important element in this financing method is the fact that the tax rate is not based on the estimated future benefits to be paid to *today's workers.* It is based instead on the benefits currently being drawn by others. This means that today's workers, as a group, are paying substantially less tax than they should in relation to the cost of the benefits that they will ultimately receive. There are two primary reasons why this anomaly occurs.

At this point in history the number of taxpayers is abnormally high in relation to the number of beneficiaries. We are benefiting from the baby boom which followed World War II and which has provided an unusually large number of worker-taxpayers compared with the number of those who have already retired. Because of its size alone, the current labor force is earning an aggregate of future benefits whose true cost exceeds the benefits that the group is currently paying, through its taxes, to persons already retired or disabled.

In addition, the average worker today is building up larger individual benefits than his retired counterpart receives. The benefits due a worker are based on the amount of his earnings that were subject to OASDI taxes. Today's average worker earns substantially more money than his predecessor on an absolute basis, and the amount of earnings subject to the OASDI tax (and therefore included in the benefit computation) is also much higher than before and is rising every year. As recently as 1965, the maximum amount that could be used in determining benefits was only $4,800 per year. Today the

4

maximum amount is $22,900 and it will reach almost $30,000 by 1981. Consequently, today's average worker is building a larger future benefit than that of today's average beneficiary.

For these reasons, among others, today's worker will one day receive much greater benefits than those for which he is now paying. It is also true, however, that today's retired or disabled person is receiving benefits that are substantially larger than those for which he paid, and basically for the same reasons. In essence, today's worker is paying his parents' benefits, and the worker's children will pay the worker's benefits when he is retired. Since in each case the beneficiary receives a windfall from the next generation, the OASDI is frequently referred to as an intergenerational transfer system.

As pointed out above, the married worker receives more protection for his tax dollar than the single person, and the low paid worker receives more insurance coverage for his tax dollar than the high paid worker. Because these and other inequities probably account for less *in the aggregate* than the intergenerational transfers described above, the inequities are frequently dismissed as unimportant. The fact is that since the windfall contained in the intergenerational transfer is quantifiable only in the total amount for all persons, the individual worker is only dimly aware of his portion of that windfall or even of its existence. On the other hand, he can easily be made keenly aware of the inequities based on marital status and income, and they may eventually influence his perception of the fairness of the entire system.

Financial Condition of the System

The cost of social security benefits is usually expressed as a percentage of total covered wages rather than in terms of absolute dollars. Using the percentage is much more meaningful because it can be instantly compared with the current tax rate and thereby quantify the potential impact on the worker-taxpayer and his employer. For example, in 1977 the cost of the system was 10.89 percent of total taxable wages, while the combined OASDI tax rate in 1977 was only 9.9 percent.[2] It is immediately apparent that there was about a 1 percent deficit in that year.

For other than the self-employed, the total OASDI tax rate in 1978 was 10.1 percent. The total covered wages, to which the tax

---

[2] *1978 Annual Report of the Board of Trustees of the Federal Old Age and Survivors Insurance and Disability Insurance Trust Funds*, 95th Congress, 2d Session, House Document no. 95–336, May 16, 1978, pp. 5, 32.

applied, were estimated to aggregate almost $900 billion. This produced about $89 billion of income together with $3 billion in interest from social security trust funds and a small reimbursement from general funds of the U.S. Treasury.[3]

As explained above, the OASDI system employs the current cost financing method. Under this approach, no large reserve fund is created from which future benefits will be paid. Instead, virtually all taxes collected are paid out as benefits to those already retired or disabled and to their dependents.

Because no large reserve fund exists, social security has incorrectly been called bankrupt and has even been attacked as a fraud. It is true that a private insurance company would be bankrupt in similar circumstances, but the government has a power that no private company has, in that it can tax future workers in order to obtain the money necessary to pay future benefits.

In spite of this, some critics have claimed that the current funding method is unsound since future benefits are too dependent upon the government's ability to levy taxes in the future. Even if the system were funded, however, payment of future benefits would probably still depend on the government's ability to tax future workers.

Suppose that a truly adequate reserve fund had actually been accumulated by the social security system. Because the system would have to cover the future benefits of approximately 110 million workers, plus their dependents, the fund would have to amount to between $3 trillion and $5 trillion. These staggering amounts equal roughly double the gross national product.

In what would such an enormous fund be invested? The total value of all listed stocks in the United States is only about $1 trillion, and all of the U.S. Government bonds aggregate less than $1 trillion. If the Social Security Administration bought all these securities, our entire society and its economy would be fundamentally changed.

The only apparent alternative would be the creation of a special type of government bond in which the social security trust could invest. But the ability of the government to pay the principal and interest on these bonds would still depend on its ability to tax future generations! Thus, whether funded or not, the payment of future retirement and disability benefits depends on the future ability of the federal government to levy taxes.

To determine the financial condition of the OASDI system, there is no better starting point than the annual report issued each year

---

[3] *Ibid.*, pp. 28, 37.

by the three trustees of the system, the secretaries of the treasury, of labor, and of health, education and welfare. This report, prepared by a group of expert consultants, projects the income and disbursements of the system for the next seventy-five years, broken down into three periods of twenty-five years each. The OASDI system is so vast that a seventy-five year period is necessary in order to foresee potential pitfalls and problems. That period is also long enough to cover the remaining years of even the youngest current participants.

The future income and disbursements of the system are dependent on many factors, but three are critical: wage increases, price increases, and the fertility rate. To forecast what will happen to these three elements in the next decade is difficult, but to predict their status over seventy-five years with any accuracy is impossible. Although the trustees and their expert consultants understand this, the estimates must be attempted to determine what might happen to the system under various circumstances. Without such a projection some long-term problems would remain hidden. Since a new study is made annually, the social security system can be modified whenever it becomes clear that the controlling factors have deviated from their forecasted behavior.

The effects of the first two factors, wage rates and prices, are reasonably well understood, but the fertility rate needs some explanation. To forecast what will happen to the OASDI system, the composition of the population during the next seventy-five years must be known. The fertility rate is the basic indicator because it represents the number of children the average woman will bear in her lifetime. The fertility rate has been on the decline for over one hundred years and was abnormally low in the years of the Great Depression and during World War II. After the war, however, it rose sharply in what has been called the baby boom, reaching a peak of 3.7 in 1957. It then began to decline, reaching a low of 1.7 in 1976.[4] (At a rate of 2.1 the population, without immigration, would eventually stabilize.) Since fertility rates are controlled by myriad psychological, social, economic, and religious factors, their future course is extremely difficult to predict.

With these caveats in mind, the trustees' assumptions about the future course of these three factors for the period from 1979 to 2053 can be examined. High, medium, and low assumptions were made. I will deal only with the medium assumptions in their 1979 report:

---

[4] *Ibid.*, p. 55.

TABLE 2
Projected Surplus or Deficit in the OASDI System

Period	Surplus or (Deficit) (percent of total covered earnings)
1979–2003	1.17
2004–2028	(0.86)
2029–2053	(3.90)

Source: *1979 Annual Report of Board of Trustees of the Federal Old Age and Survivors Insurance and Disability Insurance Trust Funds.*

- Wages are assumed to rise by gradually decreasing percentages, starting at 8.3 percent in 1979, falling to 5.75 percent in the year 2000, and remaining at that rate through the year 2053.

- The consumer price index is assumed to rise by varying amounts for the next few years and to increase steadily from 1984 to 2053 by 4 percent a year.

- The fertility rate is assumed to increase slowly from about 1.8 in 1979 to 2.1 by the year 2000 and then to remain at that figure until 2053.[5]

On these assumptions the trustees concluded that over the next seventy-five years the cost of the OASDI system will exceed its income by an average of 1.4 percent of total covered earnings. This deficit, however, is not uniform over the period, and the pattern that it follows is very significant.

From the projections in Table 2 it is clear that the financial problems of the system will not manifest themselves until some fifty years in the future. In the first twenty-five years, from 1979 to 2003, there is actually a surplus and in the second twenty-five years a somewhat smaller deficit. Not until the third quarter century will there be a large deficit. If no corrective measures are taken, that deficit will require a tax increase of four percentage points, payable half by workers and half by employers.

This peculiar deficit pattern occurs because the basic financial problem of the OASDI system is demographic and will not present itself until well in the future. The simple fact is that today there are roughly three workers for each beneficiary, but by the year 2025

[5] *1979 Annual Report of the Board of Trustees of the Federal Old Age and Survivors Insurance and Disability Insurance Trust Funds.*

there will be only two workers for each beneficiary. The smaller number of workers in relation to beneficiaries means that the workers and their employers will have to pay a higher tax rate at that time.

The projected decline in the ratio of workers to beneficiaries results from the extraordinarily large number of births after World War II, the declining fertility rate since 1957, and the assumed low fertility rates in the future. Today, a large number of persons born during the baby boom is still entering the work force and is swelling the ranks of taxpayers in relation to the relatively small number of persons already retired. Eventually, however, the people born in the baby boom will reach retirement age, and in the second and third decades of the next century they will add heavily to the benefit rolls. Conversely, during those same decades the number of workers will be relatively low because of the low fertility rate experienced in recent years and assumed for the future. Although other factors contribute to the deficit, this demographic factor is dominant.

It must be reemphasized that the accuracy of the trustees' forecast depends on the validity of its underlying assumptions. Any of the assumptions might be erroneous. The fertility rate, for example, might suddenly rise again, although advances in conception control, pronounced changes in life styles, and shifts in social atitudes point in the opposite direction.

It would be unwise today to effect drastic changes in the system to alleviate a deficit that might occur fifty years from now. Although it is important that we be aware of what may lie ahead, there is no reason to build up huge surpluses now to prepare for something that may never happen. If future events validate the assumptions, there will be ample time to make necessary adjustments.

One adjustment, for example, could be an increase in the retirement age. The 1975 Quadrennial Advisory Council on Social Security suggested considering raising the retirement age on a *very gradual basis* starting after the turn of the century.[6] If the fertility rate continues to follow the forecasted pattern, the retirement age could reach sixty-eight by about the year 2025. The concept of delayed retirement is not popular today when many new workers are crowding into the labor market every year. By the year 2025 the opposite will be true, and it may be desirable to keep workers on the job beyond age sixty-five.

If the fertility rate assumptions are correct, the society that will exist in 2025 will be quite different from that which exists today.

---

[6] *Reports of the Quadrennial Advisory Council on Social Security*, 94th Congress, 1st Session, House Document no. 94–75, March 10, 1975, pp. 62–63.

The number of children in that society will be smaller in relation to the total population. Part of the funds now spent on the rearing and education of children could be shifted to the care and support of the elderly without increasing society's total tax burden. The presence of relatively fewer children would also encourage more wives to work, and this would further help to correct the ratio of workers to beneficiaries. This latter factor has already been taken into consideration to some extent in the trustees' report. Immigration quotas can also be increased when more worker-taxpayers are needed.

In addition to these methods of handling the forecasted deficit, there is always the possibility of slowing the increase in real benefits that will occur under the present system. William Hsaio of Harvard was one of the first to suggest that the indexing of social security benefits on the basis of prices rather than wages would accomplish this objective.[7] Other analysts have also supported this proposal, which is worthy of serious consideration, particularly in the second or third quarter century of the trustees' forecast. Indexing benefits to prices will not reduce real benefits, but will merely retard their increase.

The growth in productivity, measured by the excess of wage increases over price increases, can have a significant effect on the deficit in the social security system. A significant reduction in this rate for an extended period would increase the deficit substantially, and an increase in productivity would reduce it.

The trustees have assumed a 4 percent inflation rate and a 5.75 percent annual growth in wages for most of the seventy-five-year period. In today's world these assumptions appear quite modest, and most persons would quickly accept them as reasonable. Even under these reasonable assumptions, however, by the year 2053 the average benefit being paid to a retiring worker at age sixty-five would be $306,342 per year! The average taxable wage would be $775,798 a year! Such is the power of constant price and wage increases.

To summarize, the OASDI system is by no means bankrupt merely because it has not accumulated the staggering sum necessary to fund it on a full reserve basis. With the changes made in 1977, the system should be capable of honoring its commitments for at least

---

[7] *Reports of the Consultant Panel on Social Security to the Congressional Research Service*, Prepared for the Use of the Committee on Finance of the U.S. Senate and the Committee on Ways and Means of the U.S. House of Representatives, Joint Committee Print, 94th Congress, 2d Session, August 1976, pp. 17–21; and William C. Hsiao, "An Optimal Indexing Method for Social Security," in Colin D. Campbell, ed., *Financing Social Security* (Washington, D.C.: American Enterprise Institute, 1979).

the next fifty years *if the trustees' assumptions turn out to be correct.*
This means, in effect, that if we can maintain a sound economy, with
wages increasing more rapidly than prices because of productivity
increases, the system should be able to meet its obligations until about
the year 2025 with no more tax increases than those already provided
in the existing law.

How Benefits Are Computed

OASDI is a unique income maintenance program since the benefits
are paid for by the workers themselves. In keeping with this fundamental characteristic of the system, the amount of benefits received
by a person is based on his earnings during his working life. For
persons who reach age sixty-two in 1978 or earlier, their *actual*
earnings are used in computing their retirement benefits and the
benefits of their dependents. All others will first have their earnings
indexed to the second year before the year in which they either reach
age sixty-two, or die, or are disabled. (Those reaching sixty-two, dying,
or becoming disabled in 1979 through 1983 will have a choice of
either method.) The first step in computing a worker's benefits, therefore, is the determination of his average indexed monthly earnings
(AIME). Five steps are involved.

1. *Determine the years to be included.* The base year is 1951 or
the year the individual attains age twenty-two, whichever is later.[8]
The use of 1951 as a base year reflects a decision by Congress to give
everyone a new start because many additional workers were made
eligible in that year. Starting with the base year, count all years up
to and including the year before the individual either attains age
sixty-two or, if earlier, becomes disabled or dies. Thus, a person who
becomes sixty-two in 1979 will count twenty-eight years, 1951 to
1978, both inclusive.

2. *Determine a worker's actual taxable earnings for each included
year.* A worker's total earnings are to be included for each year, but
only to the extent that they were subject to the OASDI tax. This is
an important limitation, because the maximum amount subject to tax
was quite small until recently. In 1965, for example, a maximum of
only $4,800 is includable in the computation regardless of total earn-
ings. For 1979, the limit is $22,900.

3. *Index the actual earnings of each year.* As a result of the
1977 law, the actual earnings of each year are now indexed to the

---

[8] For a relatively few people, the years before 1951 are used because it increases
their benefit.

second year before the worker reaches sixty-two, becomes disabled, or dies. This is accomplished by multiplying the actual earnings of each year by the ratio of average covered wages of all workers in the year two years prior to that in which the worker reached age sixty-two (or was disabled, or died) to average covered wages in the year the wage was earned. For example, assume a worker becomes sixty-two in 1979 and earned $4,000 in 1961. In 1977, the second year before he became sixty-two, the average wage in covered employment was 2.393 times that of the average covered wage in 1961. The $4,000 he actually earned in 1961, therefore, is multiplied by 2.393 and becomes $9,572, and that is the amount used in determining his benefits. The earnings of each year are indexed in this same fashion.

4. *Eliminate the five lowest years.* After determining the indexed earnings for each year, the five years with the lowest indexed earnings are eliminated from the calculation.[9] Thus, a worker becoming sixty-two in 1979 will start with twenty-eight years, 1951 through 1978, and after eliminating the five lowest years he ends up with twenty-three included years. He may continue to work after attaining the age of sixty-two, but he can never use more than twenty-three years of earnings in his computation. If his unindexed earnings in some years after age sixty-two exceed the indexed earnings of some earlier years, he can substitute the higher years for the lower, but only twenty-three years can ever be included in the total. Earnings for years before age twenty-two but after 1950 can also be substituted if, after being indexed, they are higher than other included years. Earnings for years after the age of sixty-two are never indexed, but they may nevertheless be higher than some of the earlier indexed years, especially because of the higher level of earnings now subject to tax compared with the lower level of earlier years.

5. *Add the indexed earnings for all the included years and divide the total by the number of months in the included years.* The result is the average indexed monthly earnings, referred to as the AIME. It is obvious that the indexing process produces a much higher figure than would be obtained with actual earnings.

Because of the new start in 1951, the system will be in a transitional stage until 1991. A person who attains age sixty-two in 1979 uses earnings of twenty-three years in the computation of his AIME, but if he attains age sixty-two in 1980 he will use twenty-four years. The number of included years will rise by one each year until eventually it reaches the maximum of thirty-five years in 1991. This

---

[9] If a worker reached age sixty-two in 1978 or earlier, actual earnings are used and the five lowest years of actual earnings are eliminated.

maximum number of years represents the spread between age twenty-two, the earliest starting point, and age sixty-two, the terminating point, minus the five lowest years.

Benefit Formula. The next major step in the computation of benefits is to apply the benefit formula to the AIME. Because we are now using indexed earnings for all who reach sixty-two, die, or become disabled in 1979 or later, the benefit formula is quite different from the earlier one which applied to actual earnings. The formula is:

90 percent of the first $180 of AIME
32 percent of the next $905 of AIME
15 percent of all AIME over $1,085.[10]

The three percentages in the formula are fixed, but the dollar amounts will be adjusted automatically each year to reflect the rise in average wage levels. This is necessary to keep replacement rates (discussed below) relatively constant.

Application of the formula to the AIME will produce the primary insurance amount, the PIA. The PIA is a worker's basic benefit and, although it is calculated as of age sixty-two, it assumes that the worker retires at sixty-five. Benefits are protected against inflation from the time a person becomes *eligible* for benefits. If a worker retires at sixty-five, his benefit must include protection against inflation from the date he became sixty-two because he could have received benefits at that time. Therefore, his starting benefit at age sixty-five is his basic PIA plus an increment that is measured by the compounded rate of increase in the cost of living since he reached sixty-two.

After a worker begins to receive benefits, they are automatically adjusted each year by the full increase in the cost of living. This is a valuable and important feature of social security benefits and is not available from any private insurer.

A worker's PIA is reduced by 5/9 of 1 percent for each month that he draws benefits prior to age sixty-five. For example, if he starts receiving retirement benefits at age sixty-two, he incurs a twenty percent reduction in his PIA. On the other hand, if a person attaining age sixty-two after 1978 delays the receipt of his benefits until after attaining age sixty-five, his PIA is increased by 1/4 of 1 percent per month of delay. There is an obvious and inexplicable discrepancy here. The worker loses 20 percent if he retires three years

---

[10] Public Law 95–216, 95th Congress, 1st Session, December 20, 1977, 91 Stat. 1514–1515.

before age sixty-five, but he receives only 9 percent extra if he works three years after reaching sixty-five.

Bias Toward Low Paid Worker. It is immediately apparent from the above benefit formula that benefits are heavily weighted in favor of the low paid worker. This point is illustrated in Table 3, where the formula is applied to two workers, one with an AIME of $200 and the other with an AIME of $1,000. Although one beneficiary has an AIME that is five times that of the other and will have paid roughly five times as much in payroll taxes, his PIA is only two and one-half times as great as that of the lower paid worker. Obviously, the low earner is receiving much more in benefits for his tax dollar than the higher paid worker.

A worker whose AIME exceeds $1,085 receives a benefit of only 15 percent on any increase in his AIME. This is a far cry from the 90 percent in the first bracket and even from the 32 percent in the second.

In 1977 Congress increased social security taxes in a very political manner. The OASDI tax rate was increased by only one-tenth of a percent in 1978. This meant practically no real increase in the tax *rate* and therefore no meaningful increases in payroll taxes paid by those workers with earnings below $17,700. Congress did, however, enact a sharp rise in the maximum earnings subject to tax from $17,700 in 1978 to $29,700 in 1981, which will raise the income of the system by the full tax rate on those added earnings. The workers who pay the taxes on wages over $17,700 will also be earning additional future benefits, but the benefits will build up very slowly and, more important, for persons who have always earned high salaries,

---

TABLE 3

COMPARISON OF THE PRIMARY INSURANCE AMOUNT OF WORKERS
WITH DIFFERENT AIMES

	AIME of $200	AIME of $1,000
90 percent of $180	$162	$162
32 percent of $20	6	—
32 percent of $820	—	262
Primary Insurance Amount (PIA)	$168	$424

SOURCE: Public Law 95–216, 95th Congress, 1st Session, December 20, 1977, 91 Stat. 1514–1515.

these added benefits will fall in the very low 15 percent bracket of the formula. In this way the high paid earner bears almost the entire burden of the increase in taxes and the system is further weighted in favor of the low paid worker.[11]

Two minimum benefits under OASDI have been part of the social security system for many years. Under the old law, a person reaching age sixty-two in 1978 could qualify for the minimum benefit if he had as little as $50 of covered earnings in each quarter for only twenty-seven quarters. The number of required quarters was equal to the number of years after 1950 and up to the year he attained age sixty-two. Thus, even though the less taxes he has paid during his working life total less than $100, a worker can qualify for the minimum benefit, now frozen at $122 per month at age sixty-five, but to be increased annually by the cost of living adjustment. The new law enacted in 1977 gives a quarter of coverage for each $250 earned in a year, or a maximum of four quarters for a year in which $1,000 is earned. Again the minimum benefit of $122 per month can still be earned by the payment of a relatively small amount of taxes.

An alternative special minimum is payable to those persons who have worked many years at low wages. This special minimum provides a maximum monthly benefit of $11.50 times the number of years above ten and up to thirty in which a worker had earnings equal to or greater than a certain amount. It is payable only if it is higher than the benefit produced by the regular formula, but the $11.50 will rise with the cost of living.

Double-dippers. The heavy tilt toward low wage earners in the benefit formula and the two minimums were deliberately designed to provide the low paid worker with at least a subsistence income. However laudable the goal, these benefit provisions have created serious problems, as the following examples show.

Adams reaches age sixty-five with a low AIME of $180 because he had few employable skills, worked at low paying jobs, was unemployed frequently or suffered several prolonged illnesses. The benefit formula provides him with a PIA of 90 percent of his AIME, or $162 per month. Adams is typical of the worker the weighted formula was intended to help.

Baker worked steadily for the federal government all his life

---

[11] There is another potential benefit in the rapid increase in the wages subject to tax. Some taxpayers will be able to raise their AIME by substituting later years for earlier years when the maximum amount subject to tax was much lower. It is impossible to quantify this advantage.

at a good salary. He receives a government pension of $700 per month. He was not covered by OASDI in his government job, so he worked most Saturdays in a local store because that job was covered by OASDI. He earned just enough in that job so that his AIME was $180 by the time he reached sixty-five years of age. Now he will also receive an OASDI benefit of 90 percent and a PIA of $162 per month, but he also has his government pension of $700. The weighted formula was *not* intended for Baker but the system cannot prevent his using it.

Why is Baker induced to moonlight to obtain the second pension? Because the first bracket of 90 percent is extraordinarily high in relation to the tax he will have paid into the system, and that 90 percent is applied to his *indexed* wages which are far higher than his actual wages. He really receives a benefit that is well over 100 percent of his actual average wages.

Baker could have done even better by working only one day a month for seven years. With earnings of only $50 per quarter during that period, he would have paid less than $75 in total OASDI taxes, but he would have qualified for a minimum pension of $122 a month for the rest of his life at age sixty-five.

Baker is not an isolated case. Approximately 45 percent of civil service annuitants receive OASDI benefits as well as their federal pension, as do many employees of state and local governments. They take advantage of a part of the OASDI system that was never intended for workers in their situation. One should not, however, blame them for pursuing this strategy; it is the system that is at fault.

The only real solution is universal coverage for all employees. The Congress is moving in the direction of universal coverage but slowly, and obviously against the wishes of a strong bureaucracy. Under universal coverage, government employees not now covered would be unable to take advantage of the high first bracket in the formula or of the minimum benefit. Even with universal coverage, wealthy persons who can live primarily on investment income could still take advantage of the progressive benefit formula by working in covered employment just enough to qualify for benefits. They would also enjoy an added attraction in that OASDI benefits are tax free. Such persons can be thwarted only by the elimination of the large bracket differences.

For persons who reached age sixty-two prior to 1979, actual earnings, not indexed earnings, are still used in the benefit computation. This means that a different benefit formula must be used. For comparative purposes, the first three brackets of average monthly earnings (AME) in the formula effective for June 1978 are listed here:

155.38 percent of the first $110 of AME
56.52 percent of the next $290 of AME
52.81 percent of the next $150 of AME.[12]

The astounding 155.38 percent of actual (nonindexed) average wages for the first bracket makes it obvious why government employees have been willing to moonlight for its benefits.

Benefits for Spouses and other Dependents. The OASDI system provides many important benefits for dependents and survivors of a worker. The computation of these additional benefits always starts with the worker's PIA, his own retirement benefit at age sixty-five.

The collateral benefit most frequently received is that of the spouse. If a worker is retired, his spouse will receive 50 percent of his PIA upon reaching age sixty-five, and if he dies, his surviving spouse will receive 100 percent of his PIA. (Both percentages are reduced if the spouse draws benefits before sixty-five.) Surviving spouses can also receive benefits before age sixty-two if they are caring for a child who is under eighteen or who is disabled.

There are also benefits for children, for parents, and even for divorced wives. In all cases, the benefit is a percentage of the worker's PIA. Because one family may contain several dependents, each entitled to a benefit, there is an overall benefit limitation known as the family maximum. It varies between 150 percent and 185 percent of the worker's PIA.

The 50 percent spouse's benefit at age sixty-five and the 100 percent surviving spouse's benefit are awarded even though the spouse has not worked in covered employment and has paid no OASDI taxes. By these benefits the social security system simply recognizes that a couple needs more to live on than a single person and that a wife will need help after her husband dies. This generosity, however, creates a troublesome inequity.

Consider the case of a wife who works after her children are raised. By working twenty years and paying the OASDI tax on her

---

[12] On July 1, 1978, the cost of living increase in social security benefits was 6.5 percent. From July 1977 to June 1978 the percentages allowed had been 145.90 percent of the first $110, 53.06 percent of the next $290, and 49.58 percent of the next $150 of average monthly earnings. (*Staff Data and Materials Relating to Social Security Financing*, Committee on Finance, U.S. Senate, Committee Print, 95th Congress, 1st Session, June 1977, p. 5.)

earnings she qualifies for her own PIA of $150 per month. Her husband's PIA, however, is $400 per month. When she reaches sixty-five, therefore, she receives $200, which is 50 percent of her husband's PIA, and if she survives him she receives $400. She gets nothing for the OASDI taxes she paid during her working career because she would have received the $200 and the $400 even if she had never worked.

Actually, the social security system has treated her individually quite well by giving her a greater benefit than she actually earned. Her treatment by the system appears inequitable only when compared with the benefits given to the wife who never worked at all. The nonworking wife is treated so generously that the working wife seems cheated by comparison. Since approximately 50 percent of all wives now work, this problem has become very widespread. It is discussed again in Chapter 2.

Retirement Test. If a person continues to work after he qualifies for benefits, he will lose all or part of his benefits in any year in which he earns more than a specified amount. For the year 1978 that amount was $4,000 for those over sixty-five and $3,240 for others. This $4,000 was raised to $4,500 in 1979 and will arbitrarily rise each year until it reaches $6,000 in 1982. Thereafter it will rise in proportion to the increase in average wages. For each two dollars that the beneficiary earns above the specified amount, he loses one dollar in benefits. Thus, if a person over sixty-five had a benefit of $3,000 in 1978 and earned $6,000 he would have had his benefit reduced by $1,000 (half the difference between $6,000 and $4,000). His total income would have amounted to $8,000, made up of $6,000 of earnings plus his reduced benefit of $2,000.

This retirement test is a cause of endless complaint. It discourages retirees from working, and it flies in the face of the concept that the benefits have been paid for and should therefore be received as a matter of right. The test had been justified on the grounds that the benefits are designed to replace earnings lost because of retirement, and if the earnings have not been lost, the benefits should not be paid. This justification is rebuttable on several grounds.

The concept of replacing lost earnings is invalid because in many cases the earnings are not lost, but are voluntarily renounced. Two persons may be perfectly capable of working, but one may choose not to do so. One obtains benefits; the other does not. Furthermore, benefits can be received after age seventy-two regardless of earnings although there is no logical reason for this distinction between sixty-five and seventy-two.[13] In addition, a beneficiary can have unlimited income from dividends, royalties, rents, and the like, and still receive his full benefit. Why should the system discriminate on this point between those who earn their income and those who receive it from investments?

The real justification for the test is economic. It has been estimated that to eliminate the retirement test would increase the annual cost of the system by $6 or $7 billion. Furthermore, the people who would benefit are by no means the most needy. For example, a person still working, with a benefit of $3,000, would lose none of this benefit until his earnings exceed $4,000. At this point he would have a total income of $7,000, including his benefit and his earnings. He would not lose his entire benefit until his earnings exceeded $10,000. The social security system is still trying to raise its average benefit above the poverty line and is not anxious to increase the cost of the system by increasing the benefits of those who already have substantial incomes.

The retirement test remains in the system for these purely pragmatic reasons. Very unpopular and difficult to justify logically,[14] it will probably be phased out eventually, but this will be done gradually in order to ease the financial strain on the system.

Effectiveness and Adequacy of the System

The OASDI system has unquestionably become the most important source of income for elderly people. Approximately 90 percent of all persons over age sixty-five are now eligible for benefits, and social security checks account for more than half the total income of 56 percent of the elderly couples and of 73 percent of the single persons who are receiving benefits.[15] Without the system many elderly people would be in dire financial straits.

But just how adequate is it to date? The average monthly benefit received in 1978 by a retired person was about $260. If the spouse was also over sixty-five, the couple received about $390. These are the averages. Some retired beneficiaries received substantially less than these amounts, and some received much more, up to a maximum of $735 for a qualifying couple. About 60 percent of workers start

---

[13] Starting in 1982, persons can receive full benefits at age seventy.

[14] See Marshall R. Colberg, *The Social Security Retirement Test: Right or Wrong?* (Washington, D.C.: American Enterprise Institute, 1978).

[15] Bureau of the Census, *Current Population Survey* (March 1977).

drawing benefits before sixty-five, thereby reducing the amount they could have received had they waited until sixty-five.

These benefit figures can be compared with the estimated poverty level figures for 1978, which were $257 per month for an elderly person living alone and $323 for a couple.[16] The average OASDI benefit is therefore right on the poverty level for an individual, but above it for a couple.

These figures, however, tell only part of the story. In 1976, 66 percent of all couples over sixty-five had additional income from assets they owned, 41 percent had earnings from work they performed, and 28 percent received private pension payments.[17] Although some couples benefited from more than one of these sources of income, others had only their social security checks. While the statistics are somewhat lower for individuals living alone, reflecting the fact that today half the aged poor are women living alone, it is clear that a large percentage of beneficiaries have other sources of income, which, when added to their OASDI check, are sufficient to lift the total income of the beneficiary above the poverty level.

Stated another way, in 1976 there were 3.3 million persons over age sixty-five who were counted as poor.[18] Without the OASDI program, it is estimated that 10 million persons over age sixty-five would have been counted as poor. Almost 7 million elderly were raised above the poverty level by their OASDI payments.

The average benefit is constantly rising, even after inflation is taken into account. The standard of living of the average beneficiary can be expected to improve each year and, if the definition of the poverty level does not rise even more rapidly, the average benefit will always exceed that level.

Replacement Rates. An important measure of the adequacy of OASDI is the replacement rate it provides. The replacement rate expresses the relationship between the benefit received by a worker and his earnings just prior to retirement or disability. For example, a person who earned $600 per month just before retiring, and who received a $300 monthly benefit, has a replacement rate of 50 percent.

The benefit formula is tilted so steeply toward the low paid

---

[16] Estimated by Social Security Administration by reference to preliminary 1977 levels adjusted by the increase in the consumer price index for 1977–1978 assumed in the January 1977–1978 U.S. budget documents.

[17] Current Population Survey, March 1977; and Social Security Administration, *Income of the Population Aged 60 and Older, 1971*, Staff Paper no. 26, table 10.

[18] Office of Research and Statistics of the Social Security Administration, paper written for Quadrennial Advisory Council, April 27, 1978.

worker that replacement rates vary materially with average wage rates. In this consideration, as in most modern analyses, three levels of wages are assumed:

- *Low*—earnings near the federal minimum wage throughout the working life ($5,512 in 1978)
- *Average*—earnings at the average annual wage level throughout the working life ($10,488 in 1978)
- *Maximum*—maximum taxable earnings under social security throughout the working life ($17,700 in 1978).

Table 4 shows the replacement ratios for these three earning levels, with retirement at age sixty-five in the years shown. For a worker whose wife is also sixty-five, these ratios are increased by 50 percent. Thus, a low paid worker and his wife would have a replacement ratio of about 90 percent in 1979 and about 80 percent in the year 2000. At that point the benefit of any couple with a reasonable work history should be above the poverty level.

The low paid worker receives a substantially higher replacement ratio than the other two, but he still receives a lower absolute benefit because of the low base to which the ratio is applied.

Because of an error made by Congress in enacting the method

TABLE 4
SOCIAL SECURITY REPLACEMENT RATIOS

Year Reaching Age 65	Level of Earnings (percent)		
	Low	Average	Maximum taxable
1979	59.1	47.4	35.3
1981	59.4	48.1	28.9
1983	52.1	41.3	23.2
1985	51.9	41.1	23.3
1990	52.3	41.4	24.1
1995	52.4	41.5	24.7
2000	52.6	41.7	25.7

SOURCE: Unpublished tables prepared by Steven F. McKay, Office of the Actuary, Social Security Administration.

by which benefits were protected against inflation, replacement ratios of OASDI would have risen steadily over the years and eventually would have exceeded 100 percent for many workers. Congress corrected this error in 1977 by changing the benefit formula to its present form, which will hold replacement ratios steady once they have stabilized. As can be seen in Table 4, they will drop sharply and then recover somewhat. This pattern of behavior results from the decision of Congress to correct the original error by reducing replacement ratios below the levels reached in 1979–1981.

The reduction in the replacement ratio for the maximum wage earner shows a more erratic pattern than for the other two, but it will eventually stabilize at about 28 percent. The reason for this deviate behavior is largely attributable to the sharp ad hoc increases in the maximum level of earnings subject to the payroll tax over the next three years. In computing the replacement ratio for the maximum worker, the benefit is divided by the maximum covered wage. The maximum covered wage jumps arbitrarily and sharply from $17,700 in 1978 to $29,700 in 1981, but the benefits rise at a much slower rate. This will drastically reduce the replacement ratio by 1982, but thereafter it will rise gradually to about 28 percent early in the next century.

Are these replacement rates adequate? The answer depends on the purpose of the system. If the system is to provide a basic minimum income, it is more than adequate for the middle and upper earner, even though for him the replacement rates range between 26 and 42 percent. For the low paid worker living alone, the ultimate replacement rate of 52.6 percent yields a benefit that is too low. Nevertheless, if he has a spouse over 65, the couple's replacement rate will rise to almost 80 percent, which should provide close to a basic minimum income because of the general reduction in living costs after retirement.

If the objective of OASDI is to permit a retiree to live after retirement with little or no change in his life style, the benefits are inadequate at the upper levels of earnings. For a low paid worker with a spouse over sixty-five, the replacement rate of almost 80 percent will probably permit an unaltered life style, but that style is already borderline. A single person with a low wage level will probably see further deterioration in his already poor existence. Although some believe that OASDI should aim for an unaltered life style, the system was not intended to achieve this and cannot do so in its present form.

The replacement rates in Table 4 assume that the worker has had fairly steady employment throughout his life. Persons with excessive periods of unemployment would have lower replacement ratios.

Other Supportive Systems

When the social security system was established in 1935, no other supportive system was available except for general welfare. This is no longer the case. Employers of all kinds have created a broad system of private pensions that cover about 45 percent of all workers, a majority of whom are employed under union bargaining contracts.

The most important new government program is the Supplemental Security Income plan (SSI). Made effective in 1974, it is designed to assure a minimum income to every person who is over sixty-five or is blind or disabled. It differs from social security in that the applicant must demonstrate that he needs the benefit because his income and assets are below established maximums, but he need never have worked or paid taxes to be eligible.

The SSI benefit in 1978 was $189 a month for a single person and $284 for a couple without other income.[19] These persons would also qualify for the food stamp program which, together with SSI, would put their income at approximately 83 percent of the poverty level.

Why the benefit is below the poverty level might be questioned, but the important point is that the SSI program recognizes OASDI cannot do the whole job. There will always be persons who are unable to develop even a minimum post-retirement income from accumulated savings, private pensions, or OASDI benefits. The SSI plan, supplemented by the food stamp program, is designed to assist these persons.

Another important government program is the Aid to Families with Dependent Children (AFDC). It does for the children of disabled or deceased workers what SSI does for the disabled or elderly worker and his spouse.

SSI, food stamps, and AFDC all require proof of the beneficiary's need. Some analysts find this objectionable on the ground that it is demeaning to the applicant. To avoid this demeaning process they would have OASDI perform the entire job of income replacement.

Impact on Capital Formation

The OASDI system has a definite effect on capital formation in this country. The intense debate now raging on the subject centers on the nature and extent of that effect.[20]

---

[19] *Social Security Bulletin* (November 1978), p. 1.

[20] See Robert J. Barro, *The Impact of Social Security on Private Saving—Evidence from the U.S. Time Series*, with a reply by Martin Feldstein (Washington, D.C.:

If the OASDI system did not exist, workers would then be free of paying some $45 billion per year in payroll taxes. Without OASDI, welfare costs could be expected to rise and some workers would make supporting gifts to their parents. These factors would absorb a large part of the $45 billion. Even allowing for this, a substantial number of taxpayers could be expected to save at least a part of the $45 billion and to invest it in stocks, bonds, insurance, and other forms of investment. This would increase the formation of capital in contrast to the social security system which simply transfers funds to beneficiaries who are spenders rather than savers.

Workers with low earnings would probably save little or none of the tax funds, because they need every penny to maintain a minimum existence. The OASDI taxes they now pay are a form of involuntary saving that most would abandon if given the opportunity. The system was, in fact, created specifically to force persons who might otherwise not do so to save for their old age.

On the other hand, many workers with annual earnings in excess of, say, $12,000 would have some discretionary income and could be expected to save at least a portion of the OASDI taxes they did not pay. They would recognize the necessity of providing for their own retirement if OASDI were no longer available, and their income would be sufficient to permit savings which would swell the fund of capital in this country.

Employers would also be relieved of the responsibility of paying payroll taxes to OASDI, which in 1978 amounted to about $45 billion. Again, part of that amount could be "lost" through heavier welfare taxes, or similar expenses. Employers could be expected, however, to use at least part of these funds to establish or expand private pension plans or to increase the wages of the workers. Either action would augment private savings and consequently result in increased capital formation.

The 1977 law drastically increased the maximum earnings subject to the payroll tax from $17,700 in 1978 to $29,700 in 1981. This step is especially vulnerable to criticism because of its impact on saving and

American Enterprise Institute, 1978); Michael R. Darby, *The Effects of Social Security on Income and the Capital Stock* (Washington, D.C.: American Enterprise Institute, 1979); Martin Feldstein, "Social Insurance," in Colin D. Campbell, ed., *Income Redistribution* (Washington, D.C.: American Enterprise Institute, 1977), pp. 71–97, 113–24; Martin Feldstein, "Social Security, Induced Retirement, and Aggregate Capital Accumulation," *Journal of Political Economy*, vol. 82 (September–October 1974), pp. 905–26; Selig D. Lesnoy and John C. Hambor, "Social Security, Saving, and Capital Formation," *Social Security Buletin*, vol. 38 (July 1975), pp. 3–15; and Alicia H. Munnell, *The Effect of Social Security on Personal Saving* (Cambridge, Mass.: Ballinger, 1975).

capital formation. The social security law was enacted to force everyone to save for his old age and is clearly necessary in the case of low wage earners. When it is applied to earnings at the new high levels, however, it is much more likely that the tax is draining off funds that would otherwise have been saved and invested.

Benefits as a Matter of Right

The principal characteristic of the OASDI program, which distinguishes it from federal welfare programs, is that its benefits are received as a matter of right since the recipient is not required to demonstrate a need for them. Irrespective of income from securities or private pensions, the recipient can still collect OASDI benefits. This aspect of the system is considered desirable by most analysts, and particularly by those who believe that a needs test is so demeaning that the social security system should undertake the whole business of income replacement.

The "matter of right" concept, however, rests on the fundamental principle that the beneficiary has paid for his benefits in the form of payroll taxes deducted from his earnings. His right to receive benefits would disappear if he paid no taxes into the system.

While the employer pays half the taxes, it should be noted that economists maintain almost unanimously that the real economic burden of the employer's part of the tax is actually borne by the employee. The tax is a cost of employment, just as the employee's salary is, and it is so regarded and treated by the employer.

Can it be said in fairness that all worker-beneficiaries really pay for their benefits?

As already explained, the earned income credit gives certain workers an income tax refund that offsets their OASDI taxes in whole or in part. In 1979, qualifying workers with less than $5,000 in earnings will pay nothing for their OASDI benefits, and those with earnings between $6,000 and $10,000 will pay less than the full amount.

The greatest weakness in the "claim of right" concept lies in the broad disparity of amounts paid by various classes of workers. It has been shown that the low paid worker obtains for his tax dollar much more than the high paid worker and that the single worker obtains less protection for his tax dollar than the married worker.

A recent study by Orlo Nichols and Richard Schreitmueller, of the Office of the Actuary of the Social Security Administration, offers a more quantified comparison of the various discrepancies in the system. They compare the present value of a worker's total future OASDI tax payments with the present value of future OASDI benefits to be gained. This comparison is called the future value ratio and has been calculated for various types of workers at various age and salary brackets.[21]

For example, a twenty-two-year-old worker today, who will always have median earnings and who remains unmarried, would have a future value ratio of 1.41, which means that the present value of his future OASDI benefits is 1.41 times the present value of the OASDI taxes he will pay. Some readers might conclude from this that he will get his money's worth, but this conclusion ignores the equal amount of taxes the employer will pay into the system. To come out whole the employee should have a ratio of 2.0 or better.

A condensation of the total results is shown in Table 5, which graphically demonstrates the heavy tilting of the benefit scale in favor of the low paid worker. The most accurate representation of the bias comes at age twenty-two, where the very low earner has a value ratio three times that of the maximum earner, whether the worker is a married or single male or an unmarried female. This example emphasizes the great discrepancy in the right of various workers to say they paid for their benefits.

The OASDI taxes of an unmarried male of twenty-two, with maximum earnings, have a value ratio of 0.92, meaning that he fails to get back even his own tax money, to say nothing of his employer's. He has therefore more than paid for his benefits. At the other extreme we find the married male of fifty-two with very low earnings, meaning a part-time worker or double-dipper. He has a value ratio of 11.78, or nearly thirteen times that of the unmarried male of twenty-two with maximum earnings. The older worker receives benefits that are worth almost six times as much as the tax payments of both himself and his employer. This does not mean, however, that all of his excess benefit is being subsidized by workers such as the one with a value ratio of 0.92. A large part comes from the intergenerational transfer discussed earlier.

Anyone with a ratio of 2.0 or more will receive benefits of equal or greater value than that of the taxes paid by him and his employer. It is important to recognize, however, that the table does not balance, meaning that the number of persons with a ratio above 2.0 is not offset by the group with a ratio below 2.0. The reason for this imbal-

---

[21] Orlo R. Nichols and Richard G. Schreitmueller, "Some Comparisons of the Value of a Worker's Social Security Taxes and Benefits," *Actuarial Note No. 95* (Washington, D.C.: Social Security Administration, April 1978).

TABLE 5
FUTURE VALUE RATIOS FOR WORKERS BECOMING COVERED IN 1978

Age on January 1, 1978	Earnings		
	Very low	Median	Maximum
Unmarried male			
22	2.81	1.41	0.92
37	3.60	1.92	1.32
52	5.27	3.08	2.14
Married male			
22	6.33	3.20	2.10
37	8.25	4.39	3.02
52	11.78	6.83	4.74
Unmarried Female			
22	3.80	1.90	1.25
37	4.92	2.62	1.80
52	6.80	4.12	2.87

SOURCE: Orlo R. Nichols and Richard G. Schreitmueller, "Some Comparisons of the Value of a Worker's Social Security Taxes and Benefits," *Actuarial Note No. 95* (Washington, D.C.: Social Security Administration, April 1978), table 1, p. 10.

ance lies in the intergenerational transfers which are received by all workers. As pointed out earlier, the present tax rate is too low in relation to the benefits being earned by the present working population, because the tax rate is geared to the much lower benefits being paid now to those already retired. The deficit created by the low tax rate will be made up by the tax payments levied on future generations.

It is even more significant, then, that some workers are receiving less in benefits than the taxes they are paying, because they are paying too low an amount to begin with. If everyone were paying a tax geared to the future benefits being earned by his own generation, the number of persons with a value ratio below 2.0 would be substantially higher.

Above all, Table 5 conclusively demonstrates that many beneficiaries are really paying for only a small part of their benefits and others are paying more than their share. All are being helped by the intergenerational transfers, but, even though concealed by such transfers, the discrepancies between different classes of current workers remain.

The subject is obviously complicated, and at present the workers themselves are almost totally unaware of these differences, except perhaps in very general terms. If the disparities increase and the general public becomes more aware of them, a movement could develop to introduce a needs test for some classes of beneficiaries for whom the system will be perceived as a form of welfare.

Minorities. It was formerly thought that blacks were discriminated against by the system. Strong arguments appeared to support this view. Statistics established that blacks had a shorter life expectancy than whites and therefore a shorter period of retirement benefits, they entered the work force earlier than whites and presumably paid taxes over a longer period of time, and they had lower average earnings and therefore lower benefits.

It is now known that there are offsetting factors. For example, blacks receive more help from the survivors benefit program than whites, since survivors comprise 29.3 percent of total black beneficiaries but only 21.9 percent of white beneficiaries. Blacks also receive more help from the disability program, since disabled workers and their dependents comprise 22.6 percent of black beneficiaries compared with only 13 percent for white beneficiaries.[22]

In short, though blacks are disadvantaged by the mortality difference, when their relatively high participation in other phases of the system is considered, the benefits payable on a black worker's wage record are found to be somewhat higher than those paid on a white worker's wage record.

---

[22] Unpublished data from Office of Research and Statistics, Social Security Administration.

2

Critique and Suggested Changes

The flaws in the OASDI system stem primarily from having forced it to serve more purposes than it can properly handle. This has escalated the costs of the system to the point where the low paid worker can no longer carry his share of the tax burden. In attempting to lighten his load the system has gradually acquired many characteristics of a welfare program and has deviated from the fundamental concept on which it was based.

It is understandable that OASDI was asked to attain extraneous social goals during its early years because alternative systems capable of achieving them did not then exist. As this is no longer the case, another rationale has now been put forth. It is argued that OASDI must continue to serve this variety of goals, because benefits are received from OASDI as a matter of right whereas benefits from other systems (SSI, AFDC) can be obtained only by a degrading means test.

There is a basic error in logic here. Benefits are not received as a matter of right simply because they are received from the OASDI; they are received as a matter of right only when the beneficiary has *paid* for them in substantial part. The fallacy lies in the subconscious tendency to assume that all benefits received from OASDI have been paid for. Although that may have been the original intent of the system, today, as already explained, some beneficiaries are paying nothing toward their future benefits, and many are paying only a trivial amount in comparison with the benefits received.

The Income Replacement System

The changes that are proposed here for OASDI are in no way intended to reduce the total help offered to the truly needy. The changes are

29

intended simply to channel that help through forms and agencies that can best achieve the desired goal and supply the greatest help to those at the bottom of the economic scale.

To begin with the most elemental principles, most would agree that today our society must provide a basic minimum income to persons who are too old to work or who are disabled. We cannot ignore such persons even if their inability to support themselves is their own fault. The question is not whether society *must* provide a guaranteed basic minimum income, but only *how* to provide it effectively and at the least overall cost.

The cost element is essential, because, like all societies, ours is one of finite resources. If even the most basic programs are to be implemented, those resources must be used as efficiently as possible. We simply cannot do everything we might wish.

It is also essential that OASDI be viewed as only one part of an overall income replacement system, which should encompass three parts: voluntary savings, involuntary savings, and supplemental support systems.

Voluntary Savings. The traditional source of income replacement is voluntary savings by individuals, usually invested in stocks, bonds, bank accounts, insurance, and real estate. Also included in this category, and rapidly increasing in importance, are private pension systems, now providing coverage for 45 percent of all workers. Although part of the cost of private pensions is apparently assumed by employers, the real economic cost is borne by the employee because the employer considers pension costs as a cost of the worker's services just the same as the worker's base salary. Far from being forced on the employee, pensions are sought and even demanded by the workers. Consequently, they are rarely involuntary in the economic sense.

Voluntary savings are essential to the economy because they are a significant source of the nation's capital. The income replacement system should be designed so as not unduly to discourage private saving.

Involuntary Savings. The second part of an income replacement system is the compulsory "saving" required by OASDI in the form of payroll taxes. Since society has guaranteed a basic minimum income to retirees and the disabled, it has a right to guard itself against those who fail to save voluntarily during their working lives and become public charges in their later years. In return for the taxes paid, OASDI should provide an adequate basic minimum income to any worker who has worked, say, thirty-five years.

30

OASDI is a program in which the worker-beneficiary undertakes to pay for his own benefits, and the benefits of each worker are related to the taxes he pays on his earnings. Since he is aware of this general relationship between his taxes and his benefits, the worker feels a sense of responsibility for the soundness of the system. If this relationship is weakened or destroyed by forcing the system to provide benefits with little or no contribution from the worker, it will lose its special character and be perceived as just another welfare system.

Because OASDI forces workers to save for their retirement or disability, its scope is necessarily limited. If low paid workers are required to save too much, we will induce the very privation that OASDI is designed to prevent. OASDI must therefore be limited to its fundamental task of providing a basic minimum income for retirees after a full working life. It can discharge this task without imposing an excessive tax burden.

Supplemental Support Systems. There will always be those who receive insufficient income from the first two parts of the income replacement system. They may earn too little to save voluntarily, and they may not be covered by a private pension system. Their work record may also be insufficient under the OASDI system to provide adequate benefits from that program.

Such persons cannot be ignored. They must be helped, but that help must come in whole or in part from other programs. That is the rationale for supplemental programs such as SSI, food stamps, and AFDC. No brief is presented for these particular programs, but whatever form they take, they should be designed to supply what is lacking in voluntary private savings and social security in order to provide a basic minimum income for all retired or disabled persons. To attain this goal might well require modification of the present programs or the introduction of new ones.

The benefits of supplemental programs should not be viewed as earned by the beneficiary, nor should the amount be related to his earnings. These programs should therefore be funded from general revenues and not from a payroll tax. A means test should be applied to make certain that only the deserving receive benefits. There has been a tendency to try to help low paid or sporadic workers through OASDI by tilting the benefit scale farther toward them and by using minimum benefit plans. These steps have progressively bent the system toward welfare and have incidentally increased the windfall already received by double-dippers and other unintended beneficiaries.

The various supplemental programs can provide low income workers with the same amount of assistance and can do this without destroying the basic character of OASDI or rewarding those who are not intended to benefit from the system.

This, then, is the general concept. Society will provide a basic minimum income to everyone, and it will be funded from three sources: voluntary saving, involuntary saving, and supplemental systems. Each source has its own special characteristics and plays its own special part in producing the desired result at the least cost to society. At present OASDI has encroached on the other two areas of the program, and by so doing is in danger of becoming another welfare system and of reducing capital formation. The changes described below should correct this drift.

Remove Medicare from Social Security

Without in any way criticizing the function and merits of Medicare, I think it should not be combined with OASDI. Since Medicare is not an income maintenance program nor are its benefits in any way related to earnings, it should be funded by general revenues, not by a payroll tax, and should eventually become a part of our national health plan. It is combined with the OASDI program only through expediency and administrative convenience. Removal of Medicare from the social security system would immediately reduce the present payroll tax by one full percentage point for each worker and each employer and in the future would eliminate the increase of 0.45 percent in the payroll tax for Medicare already in the law.

Eliminate the $122 Minimum Benefit

This minimum benefit was essential to the overall plan before programs like SSI, food stamps, and AFDC were devised. It is no longer needed because SSI now offers a larger minimum income to anyone over sixty-five and to the blind or disabled. Food stamps and AFDC are also available, and the combination with SSI should be structured to provide the qualifying beneficiary with the basic minimum income that the OASDI system provides for those with an adequate work history.

Retention of the minimum benefit is defended on the ground that it is received as a matter of right, whereas a needs test is required to receive benefits from SSI. It has already been demonstrated that today's minimum benefits under OASDI can be obtained by paying so small an aggregate payroll tax that in many cases it is unrealistic to pretend that the recipients have really paid for their benefits. If they have not paid for their benefits there can be no objection to asking for proof of their need. Eliminating the OASDI minimum would hurt only the double-dippers and others who beat the system.

Change the Spouse's Benefit

When the spouse's benefit was added in 1939, it substantially increased the cost of the system since no corresponding increase in the payroll tax was levied to pay for it. That cost-income imbalance is much greater today as benefit amounts have escalated and the life expectancy of women has risen. This is an expensive part of the total program.

Creation of the spouse's benefit simultaneously created two inequities.[23] First, it added to the potential benefits for married men at the expense of those who remain single. Second, it set the stage for the inequity between working and nonworking wives. In 1939 these problems were brushed over because it was assumed that most men would eventually marry and that only a relatively small number of married women would work. Today, however, 50 percent of all wives work, and the clamor for a fairer system has grown proportionately louder. There are now as many women "hurt" by the spouse's benefit as are helped.

Some groups have pushed for continuing the spouse's benefit and, in addition, giving working wives the benefit they actually earn. Others have asked that nonworking wives be granted a wage credit for their homemaking services. Both proposals would add to the already high cost of the OASDI system.

The logical solution to this problem is to eliminate the spouse's benefit. This would remove all the inequities and reduce the total cost of the system. How much hardship would it create?

Fifty percent of all wives now work and earn their own benefit. Some working wives have husbands whose salaries are high, but most working wives come from lower income homes where a second paycheck is essential. If the spouse's benefit were eliminated, many of the low income families would have both the husband's and the wife's benefits to support them in retirement while both are living. Many nonworking wives with no benefit of their own come from higher

---

[23] See Marilyn R. Flowers, *Women and Social Security: An Institutional Dilemma* (Washington, D.C.: American Enterprise Institute, 1977).

income homes where the husband's benefit alone is adequate to provide a basic minimum income for both while the husband is alive.

The problem stems from the fact that the spouse's benefit consists of two parts. The first is the retirement benefit, which grants the wife 50 percent of the husband's benefit after she reaches age sixty-five. If the spouse's benefit is eliminated, the loss of the retirement part will be cushioned in a large number of low income homes by the benefits that the wife has earned by her own work.

The second part of the spouse's benefit is the survivor portion—the 100 percent of the husband's benefit the wife receives if she survives him. This constitutes a more intractable problem. After her husband dies, the working wife will have only her own usually smaller benefit to fall back on. The nonworking wife would receive nothing from OASDI, and even wives from higher income homes could find themselves in serious straits.

A compromise solution would be to treat all married couples as an economic unit. In this approach, the benefit earned by either would be considered as having been earned one-half by each. While both are living, they will receive two equal benefit checks, and when one dies the survivor will receive half the two benefits. With this change, the elimination of the present spouse's benefit can be seriously entertained.

No matter how it is accomplished, the elimination of the spouse's benefit would certainly force more beneficiaries to seek help in the supplemental systems. If those systems are properly strengthened, they should be equal to the primary task of providing a basic minimum income for all.

If elimination of the spouse's benefit, however logical, is politically unthinkable after almost forty years, at least the amount of the benefit now provided should be reexamined. It is doubtful whether the benefit at age sixty-five, which now stands at 50 percent of the worker's benefit, is justified. Although no definitive study has been undertaken in this area, there are indications that a lower figure would suffice, since the poverty level for an aged couple is only about 25 percent higher than for that for a single person.

Provide Only a Basic Minimum Income

The main goal of OASDI should be to provide a basic minimum income for all who have had a reasonably full working career. Today, it provides benefits that go well beyond a basic minimum. In fact, there has been a strong effort to make OASDI the primary, almost the sole, source of all retirement income. This has had two undesirable effects. First, it has increased the cost of the system to the point that the low paid worker can pay so small a part of his share that his benefits can no longer be viewed as earned and consequently received as a matter of right. Second, though the OASDI system will always reduce capital formation to some degree, to the extent it tries to provide more than a basic minimum income, its unfavorable impact on capital formation will be that much greater.

The justification for the enforced saving program of OASDI is society's tacit guarantee of a basic minimum income even to the profligate. Having provided the guarantee, society has a right to insist that each citizen do his share toward funding that guarantee while he is capable of working. Society's mandate to save is directed to all workers, not just to the low paid worker who probably would not save anything unless compelled to do so. Even a high paid worker may fail to save during his working years unless he is required to do so.

But why should society force anyone to save more than is necessary to provide the basic minimum income? Saving beyond that point should be voluntary. We know everyone will need the basic minimum, but who is to say how much more a person should sacrifice during his working years in order to have more than a minimum standard of living during his late years? That should be at each individual's discretion.

The *average* individual OASDI benefit today is close to the poverty level, which means that many beneficiaries are well below the poverty level. On the other hand, many persons receive benefits greatly in excess of that level. Before trying to make OASDI the total retirement instrument for the nation, we should concentrate on attaining the basic minimum for everyone.

As the low paid person cannot expect to receive more than a basic minimum under the present system, he will not be hurt by the proposal to provide only a minimum income. In fact, this proposal would be to his advantage because his tax burden would probably be reduced. The middle and upper earners will receive smaller benefits from the system, but their taxes will also be lowered and they can supplement the basic minimum with private savings.

If OASDI concentrated on its primary goal, and if the other changes described above were made, the total cost of the system would drop. This would produce two important advantages.

First, reducing the heavy burden on the low paid worker would permit him to pay a lower tax and at the same time pay a fairer share of the cost of his benefits. This would strengthen the concept that benefits from OASDI are received as a matter of right.

Some persons have argued that there should be no tilting of the benefit scale at all—that all workers should receive benefits directly proportioned to their tax payments. That cannot be done and still provide an adequate minimum to the low paid worker, who has worked full time for at least thirty-five years. Even if the above changes are made, some tilting of the benefit scale will almost certainly be required, and is desirable to avoid regressivity.

The important point is that there could be some reduction in the benefit bias or at least no further weakening of the relationship between taxes paid and benefits received. The drift toward a welfare system could be halted and possibly reversed.

The second advantage of the proposals is the stimulating effect they would have on capital formation. If OASDI taxes were reduced, some workers, particularly higher paid ones, would have more money to save. Furthermore, they would have more reason to save it, because OASDI would provide only a basic minimum income, and if they wished to have more income after retirement they would have to provide it themselves, either from individual savings or by participation in a private pension plan.

What is a satisfactory basic minimum income? This is obviously a very difficult question and reasonable persons will certainly differ on its numerical definition. The minimum cannot be too high without diminishing incentive; it cannot be too low without creating suffering.

If the poverty level set by the Department of Health, Education and Welfare is accepted as the established definition, it by no means implies that all retired persons would be living at the poverty line. The majority of workers would have private savings or pensions to supplement their OASDI basic minimum.

With the changes proposed above, the present OASDI program could provide a benefit equal to the poverty level for any worker with a reasonably consistent work record at the federal minimum wage, even if the tax rate were reduced and the benefit table were less tilted. On the basis of the trustees' assumptions, the real benefit levels will continue to rise over the years to come and will result in a basic minimum above the poverty line at some future date. If the basic minimum were held at the poverty line, the tax rate could gradually be lowered.

If the OASDI were to adopt the concept of providing only a basic minimum income, an extended period would be necessary to implement the new program because of the many tacit contractual obligations already made with both workers and beneficiaries. The program could probably be handled only on a prospective basis, but this only adds a sense of urgency to the proposal.

Use of General Revenues

A fairly large group advocates the use of general revenues to finance a part of OASDI. It argues that benefits must continue to rise, but since the low paid worker simply cannot afford an increase in the tax rate, general revenues must be infused into the OASDI system.

From all that has been said above, it should be obvious that the use of general revenues is at variance with the basic character of OASDI, and constitutes a clear case of providing benefits that are in no way paid for by the worker. Benefits under OASDI should be limited to those that can be supported by the workers.

In addition, such a step is unnecessary to attain the desired goal. If general revenues are to be used to help the low paid worker they should reach him through SSI or other supplemental programs that are already properly financed by general revenues. There is no need to weaken the character of OASDI further by converting it to a welfare program.

Congress has already infused general revenues into OASDI by enacting the earned income credit. This device allows all or part of some workers' OASDI taxes to be returned to them in the form of an income tax refund. It is as though the workers paid little or no OASDI tax and a direct transfer of income tax revenue were made to the OASDI system. A movement is now afoot to increase the amount of the earned income credit and to index it so that it keeps pace with inflation.

One can certainly sympathize with the difficulty of the low paid worker in paying the OASDI tax, but if he cannot pay the tax, he should not receive benefits from OASDI. He should receive his benefits from a system like SSI, which is funded by general revenues. The basic character of OASDI should not be weakened or destroyed by infusing general revenues when precisely the same goal can be achieved through a reasonable alternative.

HD 7125 .V33
801188
Van Gorkom, Jerome W., 1917-

Social security revisited /

DEMCO